CONVENIENT AMNESIA

CONVENIENT AMNESIA

Poems

DONALD VINCENT

Broadstone

Library of Congress Control Number 2020938794

ISBN 978-1-937968-65-6

Front Cover Artwork & Design by
Tana Torrent,
Used by Permission

Broadstone Books
An Imprint of
Broadstone Media LLC
418 Ann Street
Frankfort, KY 40601-1929
BroadstoneBooks.com

For Jan, Gee, & Claree

CONTENTS

Part III

PART I

Forgetting all I ever knew, convenient amnesia. I suggest you call my lawyer, I know the procedures. — Jay-Z

LUCKY CHARM

I inherited the bop in my walk from my great,
great grandpa's lashings on the farm. So in Whole Foods
I divide aisles, a modern Moses parting white seas.

You've been warned by my charm. I crush worlds like
Godzilla.
False alarm. Keep calm for I won't cause harm.

People scramble to dodge me, the monster
with the third arm. On trains, they sneak peeks,
look away, and look again at my charm

which is like Uncle Tom, too uncool to take home to moms
so in cars, clubs, and in bathrooms, we-get-it-on-because-
of-my-charm.

Hello, you remind me of a fellow by the name of Othello
and if loving you is right, I've-been-wrong-all-along-
charm.

The take me by the hand because you-want-to-dance-
charm.

Others clear throats on elevators, then
are you an entertainer questions swarm
while quickly clutching their pocketbooks. I smile
when they look and give-them-a-buck-for-the-hell-of-it-
charm.

The once you've been charmed, you-never-go-back-charm.
Staying true to my native land but love to slang the
English-language charm.

February first should be "Give a Thug a Hug" day.
Sipping Hennessy
and Remy-Martin-charm.

Prankster and intelligent gangster all-in-one.
No forty acres and a mule, but it's all good;
I still think we should Occupy-the-hood-charm.

Don't stop with the boogie-down, hip-hop music in your
McDonald's
commercial-charm.

The militant yet guilty until proven innocent, so hush, be
quiet,
can't snitch about my kind of charm.

The ones who know won't tell, and the ones who will tell
don't know.
Can't look away from it like a soap opera. All my children
raise-themselves-charm.

You knew about it but forgot like last week's newspaper
headline.
I want to whistle whimsical feelings to white women,
Emmett Till's charm.

The charm that shines is the charm that blinds.

47 Percent Plus My Grandma

Grandma
might die, so she leaves
it to the man up in the sky.
Let go and let God, she sighs
at all her friends'

        funerals.

There's no stopping

the AARP postcards & calls
from telemarketers, tombstone companies,
and life insurance salesmen,
but she sees glimpses of hope,
like dreams no longer deferred
even through the great
economic recession.
Now, smiling at all his pictures

hanging,

remembering when she thought
she, assuaged, was at the gates of heaven
because she witnessed
the first black

        president.

ONE-OH-ONE SECTION EIGHT

Algebra: let's learn less about the functions of trigonometry
and more about writing a check, filing taxes,
and breaking down the economy.

Biology: the strongest aren't the only ones to survive,
nor the smartest. So, we adapt to change and crime
to live life beyond the limit and love it.

Penmanship: write *Egypt* 10,000 times in cursive as punishment.
No recess or after-school events. These consequences
will prepare your signature for future court-appointed documents.

Trade school: hairdressers, electricians, beauticians,
develop skills for brighter tomorrows. Thanks to vocational
schools for showing us we not only succeed, but are beautiful.

Not a King's Dream

I had a dream.
No, not a Dr. Martin Luther King's
dream, but I searched for the mystery
of equality and justice and found
just us little black boys at the mercy
of big white boys in the House of Congress
preaching progress in a sweet disaster.

I woke to a nightmare of gravel
and dust-covered grass patches
inhabited by gangsters, losers,
and crackheads. Violence stemming
from corner feuds of buddah abusers
and kids in projects. I fell asleep
again with hoop dreams and nowhere

to practice. Crated rims and cardboard
backboards where the attractive girls
kept score with short shorts, modeled
and acted like actresses. Dope fiends
trudge through the streets like zombies.
I couldn't tell if I was dreaming, but
the school systems that charged tuition

offered no scholarships for the 'hood
because apparently we paid no attention
nor listened. It had to be a nightmare
because without my permission I was
regarded as a nigger from the district, our
nation's capital. In my dream, I'm 23
and have long lived past the time I wrote

my first will. At 21 they said we wouldn't make
it, so they gave us slave reparations. We buy
the new Jordans with white bottoms and laces.
Decadence is what we represent. The only success

are the drug dealers and sellers because even
if we skipped school, professors were too afraid
to fail us. Awoken from my dream by intuition

I stumbled to my knees with hands clasped
asking the Lord to grant me a few key wishes.
At the end of the day I want to still be living
for he is a savior. I begged to be man
and not color. He spoke back saying
I don't know what you're talking about
and neither do you.

Whether in a dream or a nightmare, I replied,
race is involved. 3 points for the nigger,
$3 million for the network. Our skin
symbolizes our worth. In the media,
urban news emphasizes a gun before they
recognize the good in the community
along with the fun.

Only to repeat, re-run after re-run
with the rising of each new morning's sun.

BLACK INK

I just can't keep living like this:
nightmares of the Union battles
packaged and shipped in excrement
to a foreign land labeled as chattle.

Or forcing my eyes to the floors
in nigger-colored corridors
filled with white women
because I feel like Emmett Till.

At times I picture Jim Crow foyers,
"Shall I grapple with my destroyers?"
Still—I rise stripped of my pride.
Even Affirmative Actions couldn't
bleach Michael Jackson's insides.

See Biggie, see Tupac,
see Martin, see Malcolm,
see Huey, see Garvey;
see black leaders
and their outcomes.
When I die, will I see black?
Buried in a black coffin—trapped
Waiting on Obama to address
my situation in his fireside chats.

We real cool, right?
We die soon? Right.
With public schools
teaching us how to be fools

neglecting to tell us truths,
but that 20 bag is enough
to help us get through.
Working hard

but never hardly working
as the ink dots these very pages
inequality is inevitable.
Never will these thoughts settle.

Black boy marries black girl
giving birth to a small, black imprint
forced into a blank,
white world.

Hard Times

They didn't have a year for it
nor epoch, just called it *hard times*.
Same pot that cooks is the pot
for pissing. Angelic, yet with
our own demons, birth has clipped
our wings in dishabille, stripped away.
Still chained, shackled by handcuffs,
we are guilty until proven innocent,

far from being free, so we
find the right way to do
the wrong things. We get what we need
and not what we want. Even the moon
gets its shine from the sun.
Late justice is more useless than none,
still we rise like Michael Jordan
with the flu in the '97 NBA finals.

THE EVOLUTION OF THE SIMPLEMINDED NEGRO

A history never told
Privileged folk always feel guilty
Guilty are the underrepresented
Guilty are the misrepresented
Slanging spoken words on the back of buses
In a country with no justice
  In a country with no justice
    In a country with no justice

(This record skips on repeat)

In a country that
Must be concussed
To conceive these visions
Since we don't believe in dreams
Especially those of King
  We twitter-activism and protest
    Evoking spirits of Malcolm X

Hopped off slave ships
Out of the cotton fields
In debt to the government
Making my payments
Can't forget to pay rent
Push packs to get paid
  Push packs just to save
    Push packs until the grave

Became my own master
Always been royalty
My skin is an art gallery
Painted with crucifixes
To save me
  From lynches as a consequence
    Of too much Melanin in my pigment

The ropes turn into cuffs
Cuffs are the court
Courts aren't a sport
     The only history
          You can know is your own

Everything that glitters
Is not gold
     Everything black
          Is not evil

If I am gunned down
The universities will say,
I never earned, never learned
     Say I stole my degree(s)
          (Both of them)

If I'm gunned down
or shot unjustly please
post all of the photos
     I've taken with white women
          For they shall start the revolution

Don't forget the one(s)
With Obama
From the Wax Museum
Or his cardboard cutout quoting
His support of the troops
To show I love(d) my country
     Can they love me back
          At least half as much

PHOBOGENIC OBJECT

they built me
to be filthy
black & ugly
and forever
guilty upon
the white gaze
dialect is created
between   my body

& the world
a one-way conversation
feel the crushing

weight of melanin
white is worldly
black as sin

UNITED WE STAND

Let's send troops
to patrol
for petrol
to console

our country's consumers.

Allow illegal immigrants
to work cheap
as appointed servants,
or kill the poor

as God's hired henchman.

Create hate
among race
to display
the image we portray

as made through God's grace.

In the seam
of a dream
that seems
like a nightmare,

let *US* be America.

Invisible Boy

My mother's motto: *be seen and not heard*
        no matter how absurd, never say a word,
            keep a sullen silence through my woes.

      This saying came from sorrow, and my heart
           beats & heals slow. I don't want to grow old,
                searching for the subtle peace in my woes.

           Redefine happiness – the metaphor,
     equality is a dream with no exit door,
explaining the sudden peace from these woes.

LITTLE BLACK BOY

—for Michael Brown

Little black boy don't speak
Little black boy don't reach
Little black boy don't run
Little black boy, you're the gun
Little black boy be silent
Little black boy nonviolent
Little black boy that's gone
Little black boy, welcome home
Little black boy a dead man
Little black boy can't understand
Little black boy be vigilant
Little black boys are never innocent
Little black boy for you I cry
Little black boy, you are I.

FOR MY UNBORN SON

—For Trayvon Martin

When I die, I hope heaven isn't hell.
     We're treated like second citizens,
it ain't hard to see or tell. Don't make sense –
we can't enjoy Skittles and other goodies.
It's our fault, the love for black Nikes
and black Hoodies. Stole a life, this skin color
is a curse. Sybrina won't stop crying,
tears fall, drowning in sorrows. Should I

     lie in a river and simply wade on?
No black and white issue, too many shades
of grey are gone. There's no difference
between an Emmett Till, Sean Bell,
and Trayvon. Concealed objects:
a wallet, ID card, nothing but lint

     in pockets. Not a cent.
Red and blue sirens, white
cops, dark body. Shots fired,
someone drops. The remark
is self-defense, *He was high off PCP.*
Do they inject their bullets with PCP?
Think about it— no need to lie,
     alacrity is their alibi.

BLACK FISH

— for Jean-Michel Basquiat

Even the tar-black fishes are marked
by blues, battered and venerable,
animus to the oxygen
of our human errors. Yet, the fish
still hangs still in suspense. This
school of fish was not caught,
but ate through the bait, up the fishing
line, up through the hook, hungry for
acceptance into an unweaning
and weary world. I find humor
posthumously for I am God in the gallery,
but just another fish in the sea.

A HISTORY OF BLACK PEOPLE

—after Jean-Michel Basquiat's Painting

we be the kings and queens
of ancient cities,

Pythagoras of pharaohs' pyramids
or reaping sword swingers
following the drinking gourds.

we be the soul of the blues—

can't sleep at night,
can't eat a bite
because the nation we love,
she don't treat us right.

we be a most beautiful black,
salmon-pink colored skies
in the mind of the blind.

RICHARD PRIOR TO AFRICA

Look around, Rich. What
do you see? People
of all colors, all shades,
clay brown to coal black,
doing everything.

Do you see any niggers?
Nope, because there
aren't any. Rich didn't say it.
He hadn't thought it—
we never were niggers.

Yet we niggle, use the word
to describe our wretchedness
and perpetuate it.
White anthropologists say blacks
are the original people though,

the first with thought.

District of Columbia v. Heller

new negroes   in the house
is kinfolk   in the house
leaders of the new school
of thought
thought you knew from the way that I talk
you imagine my mannerisms and way
of the walk. deconstructing and upholstering
edgar allen poe and his baby-baby cousin
jimmy crow post-reconstruction
that ford brother

don't want us
have nothing   but we are popular culture
the predominant population, *run joe, run joe,*

run joe, run joe, the policeman
is at the door. and he won't let you
go.   it don't mean a thing if you ain't got that go-
go swing. they won't let me keep that *thing*

heard the council voted 12-1 to take our protection
let the record flow
let the record show
                for the record
                    and on record
                        black power
                            was unconstitutional.

1968 Riots: Washington, DC

1.

Ding-dong, the King is gone! (Long live the King). Hear the chime, let segregation ring. U Street turned up for the turn up. Protect my *Soul Brothers*. Burn it down. Watch it glow. These little lights of mine, let them shine on the devil's front po'ch.

2.

America the battleground is at war with black people. I repeat, well, kinda— the government doesn't care about black people. Before I give a pass to trespass. What you mean forgiveness? Whiteness wipes away their sins through the power of hymns. *Umhmms* humming on the tongue.

3.

What they sayin' on the radio? Keep King's dream alive? He ain't die for this shit- hoodoo and twisted up in his grave. LBJ say, "deny violence its victory" but the crusades of hate keep winning. Aye, man. Turn that radio off. Nah, they feds calling in the National Guard from the Pentagon. White folks will repent and be gone. What they gone do now?

4.

Destroy and rebuild: the blueprint. Whitey is taking flight. (But they be back, they be back). They upset with the civil unrest and we won't rest. You asleep already. Been sleep. There's always smoke before a fire. You hip? Yeah, been woke.

AT THE BARBERSHOP

ESPN is on the television,
muted and closed captioned.
Everyone commentates from couches
about anything—the latest slain black boys,
crime, sexual abuse, domestic disputes.
These annoying analysts are silenced
when Doc Rivers sits in the chair. *I got a woman*
croons from the sound system inviting
sing-alongs from the congregation of customers
while they impersonate the blind pianist, fingers
wiggling over an invisible piano amidst the air.

Salsa steps (front to back), either Bachata
or Merengue plays. Brown barbers speak
Spanish. Hustlers intrude selling bath soaps
and plates of soul food. Discussions of rap
fuel the feuds. The generational gaps widen—

Hip-hop is crap – all that talk about gold rings
and platinum chains. We need more
consciousness to take it back, the good ole days.

Here, they make fun of the white boys who think
they're black sporting Jordans, Nikes, and trucker caps.
Ten minutes ago, I told him I wanted the usual.

All that talk at the barbershop, I wish
sometimes they'd just cut my hair.

DRIVING THROUGH ALABAMA, BIRTHPLACE OF MY GRANDMA

My grand-momma never learned to say,
yessuh-bossuh, sir. She says she only knows
how to say, "yes, sir. Police officer!" like she
is just a little old church woman from the north
in the same tone I use

in job interviews, on first dates, and when on
the phone with customer service people.
She tells me, you know what they do
down there? They say *excuse me, boy.*
I'm going to need you
to step out of the car.

MY, MY, MY

My Nigga – or
my boy or
my homie or
my best friend or
next door neighbor, who
would take a bullet for me or
just graduated (no kids) redefining the stereotypes or
homosexuals scrapping legislatures for civil rights or
brown-men seeking freedoms from South of the border
even trailer-park,
uneducated, impoverished, dirt-poor white people,
because they are the new niggas or
Niggas Association for the Advancement of Colored
People or
Bill Cosby or
half of Barack or
those rappers promoting
violence and corner wars because
America tells us it's wrong to fight for your block,
but not your country. Never forget, you'll always be my
niggas or

My nigger – or
slave or chattle or cattle,
herded through the middle passage or
learn the ways and words of our White Gods or
you *dumb piece of shit who can barely read* and if you learn,
we'll castrate and hang you from the ceiling for public
viewing or
bastard children separated from their fathers because once
you destroy nuclear families or
rape women you destroy cultures for generations or
Nat Turner before the revolt or
Frederick Douglas or
half of Barack or
all of Barack depending

on the perspective of the speaker or
my grandmother's grandparents or my grandfather's or
my grandmother's parents or my grandfather's or
my grandmother's daughters or
my grandfather's sons on both
sides of the family or
me and/or
my children.

BODY-CAMERA

This one is different, same
Struggle though. A black body
Walking, in a familiar neighbor-

                Hood.

Taser. Suicide by cop, a term reserved
For plum-skin colored bodies
Taking up the air of what conscious-

                Ness.

Leave me alone, a voice stirring up thoughts
Of Thanksgiving dinners, teaching me to
Shoot a basketball jumper. Rest in pow-

                Pow-pow-pow-pow,
                Power,
                Big cousin.

PART II

Because some things in life are better when we can willingly forget.

In It

I hate being here, like this.
Off to my right lies the nosey neighbor's house, limp,
lonely, but welcoming; Street-lamp lit streets
are the framework for this picture. During the fall,
leaves decorate the concrete. I'm in it now,
seeing mom wave goodbye. January 12th,
about 8 o'clock. Inside the car,

inside, I feel like I'm in control. The same sensation—*I know,*
I know it, it is there, there where you sit next to me, listening,
looking at my smile, saying nothing, but your face says everything.
I know that a smile can save the world. Being here:

homes don't house the children, but the streets raise them.
Impalas and Crown Victorias paint the streets with a variant
of colors. The dying trees are brought to life by the headlights of cars
in a rush, fast forwarding, as your face pauses everything—
even time! Ahead of us, what is now back *there*,

wandering alcoholics hold hands out in caution, flailing like crossing
guards as they ask cars to slow down. Right as you glance
to your right, your hair freeze frames the moment, holding me in awe
making me cause the car to jerk. I whisper that I like your hair. Descending
onto the ramp, entering Maryland, we leave the District of Columbia.

I'm with you, sulking into silence, stuck in deep thought.
I like being alone, but I love being with you here as well,
laughing at you as you sigh, claiming you're getting sick of Jay-Z.
on the radio. Upset because you know I love Jay, I put in Jack,
just to piss you off a bit. *"Do you remember when we first moved in*
together? The piano took up the living room." The deep breath
brought thoughts of marriage to my head.

No. Not me, but I am
in the moment. I take a quick glimpse of you, again, only
to find a home in your eyes. I-295 reflects out across the windshield
as the GPS says "keep right." I pass the beltway sign titled Baltimore.

I prefer riding pass the four-lane highway passage into Baltimore,
but the scenic route of the parkway is more romantic. Riding under
this crescent moon that lights the sky. The stars, the trees, those deer,
the horizon is shaped like the brim of a hat I saw at a funeral,
nothing but blackness, the blackness that chills bones,
yet warms the heart, only because you are
here. I can't help, but to let my hand slide down to caress
your knee, smirking as you jump from my touch.

I zip past the Arundel Mills exit, keeping straight and keeping
an eye on your lips. I must remain focus at all times though, so
I pull into the slow lane, paying close attention to the road.
Inside we are. And your hands, like the feet of blind mice,
examine, familiarize, and search the undiscovered braille
of a Levi's zipper. Baltimore Darling! The lights flash
and I think to myself, where the hell is our red carpet?
The stadiums light up the sky, laughing and laughing and
laughing more to myself—the Ravens lose their chance
at the Super Bowl. I turn the stereo back on.

In my mind, all the songs seemingly make sense. *"Daddy,*
where have you been" as I think back to Steve saying
"Fuck my father, son. He no good, bruh." Nonetheless,
we are here, finally in Baltimore. The BMA is where I make
my left turn. The GPS, shutoff, a gentle vibration on my elbow
signals I have a call. JW: Where are you man?
Me: I'm coming around the mountain when I come.

You giggle beside me, head resting on my shoulder. And hearing that,
I'm in it. I'm stuck in it. The lock of your eyes have barred my soul, defining
the moments we enslave our hearts to, doing justice to my affection. Slowly
turning the vehicle, still locked on your eyes, Jay-Z raps; *"straight*
to the happy ending, 'cause I don't do stories." Parking the car,
in front of your building, words were spoken. Words were heard. Words were
understood. You slide out gently tugging your pants up to the waist while
the door closes with your hair bouncing on your back
as you disappear, with me still in it and no way out.

CONVENIENT AMNESIA

She knew the procedure:
him stumbling through the garage
entrance, smelling of Wild Irish Rose,
Newports, mixed with the scent of sweat
and sex found in Victoria's Secret. Crippled
by the thought of losing love,
she forces fingernails into his biceps,
pounding his chest on top of the love seat,
wondering why it's not called a sofa,
asking question after question
only a woman knows the answers to.

I dun cooked. I dun cleaned up
this whole entire house. I washed clothes.
I dun washed the kids' asses. Even kicked
an ass or two. And Yes,
I put on that black outfit you like. I,
I dun did all that I can take. Now, where
on God's green earth were you?
What happened to us?

The husband mumbling before he stutters
like a stalling ignition, the expression
of a confused squirrel stuck on his face,
eyes filling with tears, replies, *I forgot.*
I don't know. Dear, I forgot.
Just give me one more chance.

DATING ADVICE FROM MARRIED WOMEN

(Woman in her late 20's):
I think it's hard for two attractive people
of the opposite sex to be friends.
You're handsome. Just smile,
make her laugh. You always make
me laugh. You're too funny,
be funny.

(Woman 33, engaged with two children):
My little sisters would love you and
your swag. But the three of them
have kids. You don't need the stress.
My only sister without a child
is the wildest and I wouldn't do
that to you.

(Woman 38-years-of-age):
I am so happy you came into my life.
Don't settle down until you're thirty
something. Run these streets and ruin
some sheets. I shouldn't be this
inappropriate at work, but I must
touch your butt.

(Woman, Widow, 60 Plus):
You're a breath of fresh air.
Remind me of my late husband.
If I was a few decades, maybe
even a couple of years younger,
the things I would do.I have
a granddaughter your age,
sadly she's taken.

IN DISPRAISE OF LIES

When we speak, words wade
in the city of grammar,

a metropolis of crime
and punishment.

Who can imagine justice
silent under the night skies?

The problem is that we're commas
in the wrong place, waiting

for the truth to run-on.

DREAM JOB COVER LETTER

To Whom It May Concern:

If school were football, I'd be scoring touchdowns,
but a four-year degree isn't worth much now.
Out racing coworkers faster than Jeff Gordon,
filing paperwork effortlessly like dunks from Jordan.
I've labored for free, so you can afford me.
Put through practice job trainings like an Olympic
athlete— not that I over achieve, you under expect.

Along with my work ethic inside the workplace,
I am a creative and energetic, poet-activist
who mingles with the homeless, holding up signs
that say: *For Food – Will Write Advertisements, or
For Loan Repayments – Will be Your Indentured Servant.*

If given the word and power pointed in the right direction,
I'm an expert with organizational skills, which I excel in.
Interested in using my talents for marketing your public
image. In church, I once made God look like a gimmick.

Looking forward to hearing from you soon.

POET'S PORTRAIT OF MARIE C.

Unforgettable from your first steps in
the halls of the opera's auditorium
in your pineberry-blue khaki jacket
over a perfectly, striped button-up,
collared oxford shirt with unbuttoned cuffs
I've only seen preppy rock stars pull off
screaming *'fuck me'* in the most effortlessly
ways possible. Somewhere between struggle-
fest and jet lag from this year's Cannes film festival,
could this be love at first swoon? Colorless,
soft eyes sweet as macaroons. Enchanting
like a moon when full. Are they grey, sky blue,
perfection's hue? It is sexy yet weird
to tell a stranger you've seen them in a dream
of a dream unless it becomes true.

La Seine

Such a serene scene, the tourist
Wave pedantically from boats
At me with "sticks de selfie," smiles
And video-cameras. The nearby school
Children puff cigarettes for the first
Time. I want to write this poem
In french because I am in France
La fille de mon rêves understands.

She is the muse, the calmness
Of the waves, a gentle tide, moving
Me through the city of amour
La Seine is two rivers actually
Flowing with bridges only made for feet
As I walk my way into the music of the moonlight.

Recess at Montmartre Cemetery

Life bustles on the outskirts of flair tombs
Decadent homes for the dead are heirlooms
The schoolchildren at recess jest, and wail
As the eighty-one-year-old groundskeeper
Steps over snails, feeding cats bread that's stale
Searching for Dega's resting place, the reaper's
Success is found in the necropolis. Shales
Of roses and ceremoniously feeding of grapes
My bones thrive and jive along the trails,
The bodies of France's most famous names,
Rustle in the winds, blowing cannabis smoke.
Death makes us feel alive, an orgasmic hoax.

ECONOMIC PRIVILEGE

They know someone that
Knows someone who
Knows someone that
Introduced someone to
Pay someone to
Influence someone to
Admit a white child to
college.

I know someone who
Knew of no one. Had no
Money to pay anyone
Lied to someone
Telling that one person they
Lived somewhere else so a
Black child could get a
Better education.

SURVIVOR'S GUILT

—A Bop Poem

There's a war going on outside, no man is safe
Schools are being bombed abroad and in the States
Unarmed and unequipped for what's at stake
Either judged by twelve or carried by six is our fate
Where's my purple heart from wounds from all the hate
When your son died, the family was irate

I wish I'd taken his place. He always said,

It would be me, a prisoner of war,
Prisoner to the image, all they deplore
Battle fatigued from unwanted combat tours
Think: have you ever noticed this before
After recent elections, ISIS exists no more?
Domestic terrors screaming White Power
Black lives don't matter, yet still hold valor
No dead bodies of soldiers, but black ones galore

I wish I'd taken his place. He always said,

I'd be the one either dead or in jail
I annunciate properly just to prevail
Cut my hair to get work so I don't have to sell
Drugs like big-pharma. I remove the veil
A black male wishing I could be pale
There's a war going on aside from blackmail

I wish I'd taken his place, he always said.

FIRST KISSES

—For Lucy

It would be cliché to say:
       it began this way
or that way when
they all start the same.

Two cherries, puckering,
piquant from your
       Jack and Coke,
lips rose as a flushed face.

I think: the first kiss
happened when man
licked the first female
       implying subtly

       in a complimentary
manner that she was as
luscious as the drink
before their lips touched.

The glories of the night
gone. The effects,
the morning afterwards,
still lingering on his mustache.

COMPROMISE

Between partners could be seen as the middle of two extremes
In the workplace, a settlement of differences by concessions.
In a romantic relationship, it simply screams
One partner is happy, the other practices discretion.

ONE GLOVE

It starts with mittens—then oh, shit, a single glove
cold and alone on its own stuck in mold and mud,

crinkled up in dust, cusped with morning dew
invisible to its owner.

A glove misses another glove like light misses
darkness, or keys miss locks, or feet miss socks.

They can't make it if they tried. Just two gloves,
yearning for a you and I.

GRAB THEM

—A found poem

I moved on her and I failed.
I'll admit it.
I did try and eat her.
She was okay.
She's totally changed her look.
I've got to use some Tic Tacs,
just in case I start kissing her.
You know I'm automatically attracted to beautiful — I just start kissing
them.
It's like a magnet. I just kiss.
I don't even wait.
And when you're a human,
they let you do it. You can do anything. Yeah those legs, all I can see is the
legs. Grab them by the beaks.
You can do anything.

CULTURAL CO-OPTING

define blackness: (adj) an expectation,
fabricated histories of hoodoo,
ethnic features (ass shots)
savage barbarians of black magic,
cannibalistic tendencies, backwardness,
waywardness fetishes, social stigmas,
slave traders, day laborers, niggers.

I did not create the meaning, it was
already created. consciousness
committed to experience knows nothing
of determining a being. the creator
enforces inferiority, but he needs
my sauce, my flavor, my swag.
I am a poet of this world

& in tune with its vibrations &
cosmic understandings. the creator
has discovered poetry that has nothing
poetic about it. he is locked in his
whiteness. I am black—living & losing
myself looking for acceptance,

sympathetic to the skipped heartbeats
of my generation while the blackface
man, however educated he may be
can never understand Miles Davis
or Jay-Z (pre-rap-retirement). I am
black, not because of my skin,
but because I embody struggle
defying expectation every day.

RIDING THE T

The hung-over belle, a B.C. grad student,
induces from the spider's-web of her tangled hair
veiling *A Perfect Day For Bananafish.*
She chucks up a giggle content.
Glaucous day
makes my blemished black reflection grotesque.
Chicks prattle in the handicap doorway.
Gaze! Those seconds, gentle smiles tame
as if gardens never became jungles after rain.
(This is the train for morning's "walk of shame")

What use are my sunshades?
I peek at the Boston U. biddies, who look cute in groups,
or quick glance under the influence of Samuel Adams,
(and low alcohol tolerance!)
still nursing headaches with Dunkin Donuts coffee
as they gloat, ramrods
with the eyes of owls
perched on handrails,
scouring Margo's *Nine Stories* & Starbucks cup.
A wealthy, preppy profile in a burgundy sweat-shirt,
worn this morn, slept-in at night,
she sees her image in the window,
an aging butterfly from her physical cocoon—
drowning the young girl like a terrible fish.

This is a creative space hurling us together at the Park Street stop;
third rail & human interaction, friction makes the spark…
Smorfia '17,
a replica of Margo's mother
without absence of varicose—
close to gross as the Tahr mountain goat,
as she blasts back to the present past
and urinates moody for a mate.
She thinks she's a woman, but realizes she's just a girl.

In between dreams at night,
Time never truly seems to move forward,
But we are reminded of quite the opposite
at least once a year.
(There are no one night
stands in the gates of Heaven.)

After a lustful ride on the B-Line,
I am in love like a twelve year old
this very day. Stoned lamprey,
I limp in my hipster low-rise, skinny Levi's
before the glass mirror panels of the door,
and see the shaky circumspection reflected
in the wrinkled, make-up faces
of the girls down the road a few decades.
Time is the music the planets make,
each of us carries the tune of a final note.

MAY FLOWERS

I know you might not remember
but it feels like yester/whenever—
the days, they blend together

tender as morning glory petals
cupping a bumblebee's proboscis
wiggling in the wind's breeze

taunting me with their laughter.
All we can do is hang in air, holding
onto the memories that are dreams.

PART III

To not know is not miserable. Being aware that you don't know is miserable.

TRIGGER WARNING

Is art not

capitalist propaganda?

THE AVOCADO EATERS

—After Gwendolyn Brooks

They eat avocado toast, this millennial couple.
Brunch is a bougie affair.
Upcycled cookware on vintage reclaimed wood,
Mason jar drinkware.

Two who are Mostly *Woke*
Two who have volunteered and donated time
But keep on thinking privileged, white thoughts
And gentrifying the neighborhood.

And remembering…
Remembering, with misanthropy and dysmorphia,
As they huddle over avocados in their West Hollywood
Hills homes that
        is full of La Croix and Möét Chandon and Chanel
and juice cleanses
            nose candy, blonde-hair models, and movie scripts.

A POEM FOR SILVERLAKE HIPSTERS

—after Amira Baraka

She had got, finally,
to the desert
of desire. There were no
palm trees, or prey. No Ben Silbermann
pinning decoratively
vintage dresses, Matcha tea drinks
supporting non-local business,
empowering capitalism.
Only clickbait,
engulfing you into
the algorithm– ideas
and their opposites.
Like, minimalism,
She doesn't need,
only really is told
what to want.

NOT VENTURA

—*After Kay Ryan*

Everything exists as a roadblock
and cannot be rubbernecked.
So if not on Ventura
it's not just podcasts;
it's the best-selling audiobooks.
Don't you wonder
how drivers idle
the highway lines
and time is not vital?
How we'll switch lanes,
daydreaming of sleeping
with other passengers,
the allure of meeting
on the 101 as travelers.

FREE BIRD FINALLY FLIES

—for Maya Angelou

What would the air say?
Where does a song go
When there's no one left
To sing it? Silence!

Not woman, not art,
Nor irascible, nor tart.
But Goddess of solace,

Hope takes an eternity,
And the bars of disparage
Disappeared with the whispers
Of your last breaths.

America is still a cage or
Jukebox with no change or
Shackling cackles of the radio
Airwaves on AM stations or

The chirp of unwanted work emails,
Facebook statuses of your passing,
Unwarranted, notable, and quotable
Tweets, a celebration of soul and song,

These bars are never-lasting. Hate is
A welcoming prison – liberate yourself
With the melodies of love because

Silence is you, the poet lost
In an unfamiliar tribe. The air—
An untranslatable language immune
To the minds of the anguished.

DEAR LADY BALLETOMANES,

1872–Dance Class at the Opera by Edgar Degas

Corps de Ballet
> On our floor, we are all equal.
> Bodies bending bullishly across
> the earth. We'd rather stride than
> resist the temptation of leisure.

Piqué

> Pricked position on *pointe*, balancing
> on the ball of our feet, arms flail outward
> prepped for flight. We winged dancers
> aim to land on stars with half-crescent smiles.

Penché

> Leaning into the love of life and dance,
> I embrace my own dearest on-looker.
> A leg amidst in thin air, a freezing stare
> capturing every second of silence.

Pirouette

> Limbs twirl, dizzying and distorting
> reality. Whirling and ready for the
> *Grand Jeté* with subtle stealth. Precise
> movements in real time.

Sickling

> None refrain from the fall of youth.
> Aging bones begin to succumb to the pressures
> of an incorrect step and posture. Rhythmic
> moves fading into an abyss of nostalgic dreams.

LEIMERT PARK AND NIGHTCLUBS
—after Ralph Waldo Emerson

Urban parks and street art are good by day;
I do delight
In the black-owned acres of the night,
My seasoned pre-roll interrupting
The sleeps of kin or dreams of ancestors.

ASK ME WHY I REMEMBER HER NAME*

"In her absence, / everything seemed something else"
—John Skoyles (Initials Written on a Screen Door in Dew)

when the freesia bulbs wilted, her
scent lingered over strange places, an absence
of a combination of worry & thought. everything
rarely seen not in praise of poison seemed
a secret, like faith practiced before bed. something
like poetry in the future tense, else

it be a song that stirs blood yet to flow in veins, else
it be tucked into a bottom drawer, loved & unused. her
story has been a hit record for decades, something
like *We Found Love In A Hopeless Place*, then—absence
then *I Will Survive* & *I Will Always Love You* or it seemed
she'd be my everything

i'd be her everything
nobody else
seemed
to embody her
purest essence or absence
of persistence. something

said is something
seen. everything
absent
in itself is else-
where with her
or so it seemed.

she is impressed by what is not understood or so it seems
so parts of me must remain a mystery, something
causing considerable cloudiness, the counterpart to her
beating but unflinching heart, variegating everything
at times, sometimes, most times, i wish i were someone else
while balancing the darkness of my canvas & her absence

mother earth was formed,   a formless void, an absence
of life, love, light, and all things good. it seemed
like a holiday to meet you, a holy day to know you. all else
is a sin. the memory of your scent, a consequence, something
too sweet to regret. after a— i want to be friends text, everything
changes. i am forced to think: well, what were we before i met her?

absence is a name and nothing else. ask me why i remember her
name, her favorite podcasts, favorite french film? she is everything
like hope, like prayer without god, like let's change some things.

Sestina by way of a Golden Shovel form

BIRTHDAY DINNER RESERVATION FOR ONE
—for Matthew Dickman

Because it was my birthday and I was alone
the well-favored waitress invited me
to the Chef's table for dinner.

I politely declined. Your poems
on my iPad kept me company. I wasn't alone
because you were with me.

Like cat-eyed puppies at the animal shelter
or like those dollar-a-day support systems
for disenfranchised kids, I wanted to help,
wanted to be there because you were with me
on my birthday.

I cried, dropped a single tear. You spoke to me,
Reaffirmed that loneliness is a table full of bread
and wine and you are starving, but unable
to eat or drink. I want to share it all
with you because you were with me
on my birthday.

My ex-girlfriend had finally mastered a skill,
disappearing and perfected not being with me
anymore. So, if it all feels heavy like eyelids
rolling over eyeballs, feel free to send me an email.
We'll walk to the nearest gas station,
purchase some rolling papers,
and talk stories and fairytales of poets'
mistakes at first impressions because
you were with me on my birthday.

The assess of the Jamaica Plain women walking by
the window outside kept interrupting our evening.
There's still a crick in my neck from the constant
craning up and down, watching like I'm at the zoo—

all this honey, while I just want to feed the bears.
But it was okay. It was alright because you were with me
on my birthday.

The jazz jazzed on and I understood
why you break your lines the way they do,
why stanzas stand alone
why white space occupies the page like everywhere else,
but your letters stayed with me
on my birthday.

The busboy-lady asked how my meal was
in between the courses. I told her
the first course was exceptional,
the second was bland, but it was better, actually
much better if not the best
when she came by to ask me how it was.
It became best I sip the paired wines
and hold my tongue, but she never came back.
But all was well in my world because
you were with me on my birthday.

TOM AND JERRY

Even though quitters never win,
              you always seemed to lose, quite
the catch. You had to say sorry,
              apologize for nature, your desire
to chase, capture, and eat.

So you kissed Jerry on the forehead,
then you kissed him again. And with slobber
              and drool, you put Jerry in your mouth.
Shamed and slammed up and down
for being cruel, you spat him out.

Funny how when we gain and get
              what we want, we eventually lose it.

We MFA: Poetry

—after Gwendolyn Brooks

We make reality jealous of fiction. We
exercise exaggerated diction. We

fathom the imagination. We
describe damnation. We

try to change the world with words. We
have the right to remain silent with verbs. We

place our faith in our poems. We
must pay back student loans.

BLOOD OF CHRIST

—*after John Skoyles'* Excuse for a Love Poem

Yes, it was definitely the last drink
(or drink before) that made
me feel this way—not yet loved,
but cared for like a first significant

other. It had to be the drink before
last (or maybe even the one
before that) because she began
to make sense. "Religion or sex?"

she asked. "If you can't choose one,
then you'll fall for any and every
thing. Can't stand for either, then
you are a hypocrite." I understood

it all. Her words made me drunker.
Desire there. The ability to perform,

                                        elsewhere.

TRIO OF TRIOLETS
—for Gail Mazur

I fancy shoes with red laces
to whom it concerns, sincerely.
No races, I prefer paces.
I fancy shoes with red laces.
I crave solitude, less spaces
at least yearly to see clearly.
I fancy shoes with red laces,
to whom it concerns, sincerely.

I fancy shoes with red laces
to whom it concerns, sincerely,
I'm no patient nor have patience.
I fancy shoes with red laces
severely; soles, their embraces.
Death to austerity cheerily,
I fancy shoes with red laces.
To whom it concerns, sincerely.

I fancy shoes with red laces
to whom it concerns, sincerely
faces of all generations.
I fancy shoes with red laces
for ages by God's good graces,
missing my beloved, dearly
I fancy shoes with red laces
to whom it concerns. Sincerely,

MEN I'VE SLEPT WITH

—for Matt Dickman

I carry your poems.
(I carry them in my backpack)
Always over my shoulder,
everywhere I go.

Whenever I sleep, next to my bed
or under my pillow.
Like Lady Day's crooning,
your words lull me

into a suspended stupor,
barely even conscious,
having conversations
with my consciousness

during nights of cold sweats
when I wanted to be a poet,
to have the tongue of God.
I say, I shouldn't love a man

this much. I fell for Langston,
he was by my bedside first,
thanks to his light skin.
Followed by other black living legends—

TSE, Kevin Young, Fred Moten,
Carl Phillips, but *Mayakovsky's Revolver*'s
hard cover should be wrapped
in selvedge denim, those words,

your words do not unravel.
Seemingly a prophet,
your scriptures remind me
of my ex-girl. Friend,

if Major Jackson were wheat bread
then you'd be the organic,
French baguette, top shelf.

OXYMORON #FAMOUSPOET
—after Frank Bidart & James Franco

When James Franco first spoke to me, he said, "Oh, shit. You're Mr. Hip. We were just talking about you before the reading."

•

James was humbled to be reading with the icon, living legend, and friend Frank Bidart.

•

James lives a scholarly life. A contemporary-renaissance man, he embodies the ekphrastic elements of theory. Aside from acting, directing films, and being artsy with an MFA from Columbia University, he will soon earn his PhD in English from Yale. Writes fiction and poetry, quite the nerd.

•

James' life is tough too, though. His pretty face gets objectified like visible nipples on busy Manhattan streets. So he read from *New Film Stills*, a collection of poems with adjacent photos of James dressed in drag. Still, the women say, he makes a handsome lady.

•

I stayed after the book signing to meet Franco. Mesmerized by the most beautiful woman in the room named Anna, who just so happened to work for James, I waited and spoke with Frank.

•

Donald, like Frank, very much enjoyed James' acting in Pineapple Express. Donald doesn't fancy fiction much, but enjoyed Palo Alto too.

Donald did very much love James' paintings. Even the female-gaze nude paintings of his buddy Seth. Paintings are worth a thousand verbs.

•

Say: CHEESE – Now, I am in a photo with Mr. Snicklefritz and Mr. Ellen West.

•

Why would you support that? Why would you buy his book?

I learned to never judge a book by its cover. Never assume why the words are on a page, in a particular way. Why can't a star write poetry without it being seen as trolling? What does one do?

Why can't they have something to express? Why can't I write what's near and dear to me?

•

Because my audience is not comfortable. Even though I am the page and the page is me.

James' poetry taught me this.

•

An old pal of mine asked if I could send her the photo. She reassured she wouldn't send it to anyone. She joked about not cropping me out of the photo. She cropped me out of the photo.

•

But then I posted it to Instagram. And @FrancoFan69 actually crops me and Frank out with a condoling thank you mention and something about Lana Del Rey.

•

James laughed before he responded about reading about himself in the media during the question and answer session. He said: I don't read too many reviews about myself. The last time I read a review, it was really mean. I have people like Frank that I look up to, which is all the confirmation I need regarding my art.

.

Donald knew after hearing this that James was a cool dude, knew that James was exactly the guy from the poem on page 52 of his Directing Herbert White book.

Take me, even the fake me. Our written words become us, our memories.

.

So Lucky,
Badass,
Damn,
Spriinnnnggg breaaakkkkk,
Oh ma gah,

The first woman I spoke to at the reading was there to see James. She liked poetry fairly – I had to ask. Thanks to James, she was able to hear Frank read. I told her Frank was the best.

She commented: *Frank was incredible!* I thought she was cute and had cuter sunshades. I told her I dug the shades.

.

Donald posted a few photos with Frank Bidart before, but poetry isn't popular culture. If it is, Frank is not Instagram poetry. But James; however, is.

.

Donald would learn this after posting the photo with *Frank and Franco* on Facebook.

•

#Whoa,
Living the life,
Tell him I say sup,
You just reached a new level of hip
Oh my god,
I wish I'd known about this! I moved to NYC and would have loved to
see you.

But people only want to see you after they see you with important people.
Too many, *Hey, Donald how are you doing*s in my inbox. Too many, *I'm just
seeing your last message, how are things after a ten month lapse in communication*
in my inbox.

Way too many likes on this particular photo. They like James. Some like
Frank. Most like James. Few like me. Together, this is the poetry-me.

The people love the fake you. They could've been wax figures.

•

I heard he was weird, was he weird – who isn't weird?

He was in the news for trying to get a girl from Instagram – who hasn't
tried to pick up a girl from Instagram?

I didn't know he wrote poetry. Did he read it well – I know a lot of poets
and even they don't read well. It's what's on the page that matters.

Was he high – does it matter? It's a poetry reading. We all have secrets.

•

In one of James' poems, He says,

> All movies suck. Which ones are good?
> The ones that are good, even they are no good.
> You have to like no-good movies to like movies.

This is the same for love, for sex, for people, for poetry.

•

"And after all, only Whitman and Crane and Williams, of the American poets, are better than the movies." – Frank [O'Hara]

•

Everyone loves the poor artists. Has their opinions on rich ones. Celebrate popular culture, pop-poetry, viral verses, status stanzas. Or they want to until the mask comes off. And the poets' problems are the people.

•

Art is love. Love is a poem that does many things. I don't laugh at her anymore because I am understood by it.

•

Sometimes, I don't want to be the "me" in the pages of my poetry. He is unread. He is unfelt, becoming silent language, a collection of dust.

REALITY AWAITS WHEN WE AWAKE*

—for Frank Bidart

When we don't dream, we die so
Close your eyes, sacrifice your inhibitions. Much

Of faith's understanding and meaning depends
On our mental activity, completion of tasks, upon

Movement, upon memory, a
Moment a white bus ran a red

Light. You screamed, *Jesus!*, gave Him the wheel
And your will was done. Later you filled a barrow

Full of weeds and trimmed hedges from your garden, glazed
Over from dew and 80-year-old perspiration with

Songs of *seeing the King soon.* When it rains,
It pours, Grandma. Forgetting is Sandy and Katrina. Water

Drowns the itsy spider, yet saves our soul beside
The sin of superstition, aside from questioning, the

Story when coworkers believed you were born white,
Or you'd heading Home soon & there'd be no more fried chickens.

*Golden Shovel form

AMHERST'S AEOLIAN HARP

—for Emily Dickinson

It is the instrument that transports us –
Our origins cannot be the purpose
Elsewhere but Here! thus lives are brusk.

We are flesh. Then ash. Or dirt. We are earth.
Adolescence is exceptional. Yet adulthood,
A caricature, the mellifluous instrument –

When foundation settles, floorboards creak,
The wind whispers munificent breezes
Of harmony. It is the instrument, not the sky's

Cacophony of jealousy, snaring drum
Splashes, tinctures of rain. Hark!
The vibration of its strings. Through tunes,

Meaning we can find, our Bodies weakened,
Meaningless as a toss-and-turn night's sleep.
Meaningful are risible sounds of Heaven's scent,

But listen for the slants. Listen for the scants,
Hear your body recant. Hear the harp chant.
This instrument transports us when life can't.

HE SAY—SHE SAY

—after e. e. cummings

nice to meet you said he
the pleasure's mine said she
your smile is refined said he
care to dine said she

where to said he
anywhere said she
you don't care said he
only if you do said she

a glass of wine said he
a merry time said she
a bite to eat said he
a few drinks said she

blue moon said he
chardonnay said she
tofu said he
grilled cheese said she

bill said he
i've had my fill said she
too much liquor said he
i saw your twitter said she

what's next said he
umm said she
hmm said he

are you sure said he
i want nothing more said she
alright said he
hit the lights said she

oh says she
whoa says he
oww says she
wow says he

go fast says she
how fast says he
like vroom,
vroom says she

you're the ocean says he
no poetry says she
but the motion says he

like a boat says he
sheets are the waves says he
i am saved says he

WARHOL: TO JEAN-MICHEL BASQUIAT FOR APRIL FOOL'S DAY 1987

My painting is dead.
Defend it for me, Basquiat, protect my honor.
I am not in the right place—for I am not a painter.

There's no such thing as art for art's sake,
this I promise. Artists exist to create beauty
from their imaginations and force them

onto the interpretations of others. Wallace Stevens
once said, "Let be be finale of seem," and your
art is a reflection of you—it is what it is.

My paintings are dead,
but they will live forever in the kingdom
of art and all things wonderful.

God, how I love boring things. Taking
the dull and making it shine
is how our legacies will be left behind.

The true creator, of heaven and earth
made us in his image, and oh, how
glorious his imagination awakens our souls.

Through you, my paintings are alive.
They live on. Immediate acceptance
by the world does not determine true art

for at heart, I am truly not a painter. I am
a visionary, a rebel to the norms of beauty
for it is in the eye of the beholder.

Now, I am in the right place, doodling on
heaven's doors. Art is in the subtle, below standard.
Wallace was right: "the imperfect is our paradise."

WAKING FROM SLEEP

Aspen Dream, Near Ashcroft, Colorado
—Plate 6 by John Sexton

You, like the Aspen Dream, a beautiful forest of white,
are from the imagination and chapters of fairytales that
last
a lifetime. On the floors of the Coloradan forest, I
search high & low for your lost slippers. Luckily, the sun
shines through giving nourishment to all, as you do
when you make those funny faces, that only I seem to
enjoy.

Out here, nothing can be tamed. All is wild. The aspens
stretch out bending awkwardly, seeking life from
the sun. Your figure illuminates & no matter how savage
our emotions get, one spoken word & I become docile
like the tranquility of the trees during the setting of the
sun.

ACKNOWLEDGMENTS

'Amherst's Aeolian Harp' in *A Might Room: A Collection of Poems Written in Emily Dickinson's Bedroom*

'Tom and Jerry' in *Poetry Quarterly*

'47 Percent Plus My Grandma' in *Soundings Review* (Fall 2013)

'Recess at Montmartre Cemetery' in *Literati Magazine*

'A History of Black People' and 'Evolution of the Simpleminded Negro' in *Third Stone Journal*

'La Seine' (Audio) in *Golden Walkman Magazine*

'Phobogenic Object' and 'Ask me Why I Remember Her Name' in *summer stock journal*

'Reality Awaits When We Wake' in *Gianthology (Heroes are Gang Leaders)*

'Poet's Portrait of Marie C.' (with Audio) in *Five 2 One Magazine*

'Lucky Charm' in *Black Heart Magazine* and *Black Heart Magazine's Best of Black Heart 10 Year Issue*

'Oxymoron #FamousPoet' in *Hobart Pulp*

'Men I've Slept With' and 'Dating Advice from Married Women' in *Clarion Literary Magazine*

'Free Bird Finally Flies' in *BDCwire.com*

'One Glove' in *Citizen Brooklyn*

'Dear Lady Balletomanes' in *Stone Highway Review* Issue 2.3: May 2013

'For My Unborn Son', 'Trio of Triolets', 'Blood of Christ', 'Waking from Sleep', and 'Black Ink' in *Boston Poetry Magazine*

'One-Oh-One Section Eight' and 'Not a King's Dream' in *Eunoia Review*

ABOUT THE AUTHOR

Donald Vincent received his BA in Writing and Public Relations at Loyola University Maryland and MFA in Poetry from Emerson College. He is also known as Mr. Hip, a music recording artist with music available on all streaming platforms. His music projects include Vegan Paradise (2018), Who Is Mr. Hip (2018), International Hip (2017), and Jokes From My Ex (2015). He teaches English Composition at UCLA and Visual & Media Arts at Emerson College Los Angeles. Originally from the Southeast sector of Washington, DC, he currently lives in Los Angeles and at www.hidonaldvincent.com.

Book designed by Larry W. Moore
for Broadstone Books,
using Garamond for text &
Trebuchet for display,
printed in a limited edition
on permanent paper
by Bookmobile